KFK KINGFISHER KNOWLEDG

CASTLES
&FORTS

▼ The Citadelle Laferriere was constructed between 1804 and 1817 on the Caribbean island of Haiti to protect the newly independent island from possible invasion by its former colonial ruler, France. It was designed by German engineers who were then imprisoned inside the fortress for fear they might reveal the secrets of its construction. The fortress is now a UNESCO (United Nations Educational, Scientific and Cultural Organization) World Heritage Site.

KFK KINGFISHER KNOWLEDGE

CASTLES & FORTS

Simon Adams

Foreword by
Neil Oliver & Tony Pollard

KINGFISHER

Publishing manager: Melissa Fairley
Senior designer: Peter Clayman
Picture manager: Cee Weston-Baker
Production controller: Debbie Otter
DTP manager: Nicky Studdart
Artwork archivists: Wendy Allison, Jenny Lord
Proofreader: Sheila Clewley
Indexers: Sylvia Potter, Sheila Clewley

KINGFISHER

Kingfisher Publications Plc, New Penderel House,
283–288 High Holborn, London WC1V 7HZ
www.kingfisherpub.com

First published by Kingfisher Publications Plc 2003
First published in paperback 2006

10 9 8 7 6 5 4 3 2 1

1TR/0606/TWP/MA(MA)/130ENSOMA/F

ISBN-13: 978 0 7534 0877 3
ISBN-10: 0 7534 0877 5

Printed in Singapore

NOTE TO READERS

The website addresses listed in this book are correct at the
time of going to print. However, due to the ever-changing
nature of the internet, website addresses and content can
change. Websites can contain links that are unsuitable for
children. The publisher cannot be held responsible for
changes in website addresses or content, or for information
obtained through third-party websites. We strongly advise
that internet searches should be supervised by an adult.

GO FURTHER...

INFORMATION PANEL KEY:

 websites and
further reading

 career paths

 places to visit

Contents

▼ The ramparts of Agadir, on the Atlantic coastline of Morocco, in Africa, were built in the 1540s to protect the town's kasbah (castle) and to keep an eye on the neighbouring Portuguese, who had built a fortress in the town and wanted to expand their control along the coastline.

Foreword

Castles and forts are truly magnificent reminders of our past, and that is no coincidence – they were built to impress. They were also built to last, which is why so many of them have survived to the present day, even if time and warfare have reduced some of them to little more than a spectacular ruin. These buildings inspire the imagination. As children we played with toy castles at home, while on holiday in Scotland or Wales we enjoyed exploring the real thing. Today, they continue to excite us and, as archaeologists, we have excavated in and around several of these romantic ruins.

We all have our own idea of what a castle is, and for some of us this image may have been influenced by the many books and films about King Arthur and his own mythical castle, Camelot. There are towers with fluttering flags, battlements guarded by men in armour, arrow slits in the walls and a drawbridge spanning the water-filled moat. These were safe places to which people fled when the enemy attacked, the high walls keeping back the marauding hoards. But as this book so clearly illustrates, there is much more to castles than sieges and knights in armour. For one thing, there are many different types of castles and forts, and they are to be found all over the world – Japan, the Middle East, Europe and, in more recent times, even America and Australia. In *KFK Castles & Forts*, you will learn how forts and castles first developed, how they evolved to meet the changing needs of their occupants, and adapted to technological developments in warfare, from slingshot and longbow to gunpowder.

Each and every castle or fort makes us marvel at the thought of the people who designed them, built them, lived in them, defended them and finally abandoned or were driven from them. They were centres of authority, market places, a focus for the growth of towns, and above all, impressive symbols of power, reminding all those people who lived around them just who was in charge. But on the simplest level they are places where people lived, and as archaeologists this is what interests us most about them – the secrets they have to tell about the day-to-day existence of those who lived within their walls.

But for every question our excavations let us answer, they seem to reveal yet more mysteries to try to solve. We have often found that castles protect their secrets every bit as stubbornly as they once protected their inhabitants. These mighty structures are as much a part of the landscape as the mountains and valleys, the rivers and lakes, the towns and the cities. Although they might look like they will last forever, they will not, unless we keep making sure they are protected and looked after for the generations of people to come. Armed with this wonderful book on your next visit to a castle or fort, you will be able to understand much more about why these fascinating buildings were constructed in the first place – and how they have managed to last for so long. Who knows, you might unearth a secret or two yourself...

Neil Oliver & Tony Pollard – archaeologists, and presenters
of the BBC television series *Two Men in a Trench*

Iron Age stone fort at Inishmore, Ireland

CHAPTER 1

The first forts

No-one knows exactly when the first fort was built, or where it was, but we do know why it was built. Our ancestors needed to defend themselves against hostile tribes and wild animals, so they built simple defences out of wood around their houses and farms. Later, the first civilizations in the Middle East and then Greece built fortified citadels or strongholds out of brick and stone that were both palaces and places of refuge for the local population. Most cities had walls or earthen ramparts around them, and guarded entrances which could be closed at night or in periods of danger. The Chinese even built a wall around their country!

By the time of the Roman empire, 2,000 years ago, substantial fortresses were being constructed to house the Roman legions and subdue the local population.

Bronze Age fortifications

From the middle of the third millennium BCE – when the ancient Egyptians were building their pyramids, and other civilizations and empires in the Middle East and India were constructing palaces, temples and fortified cities – Europeans were defending themselves from attack in fortified villages.

Living in fear

The people who lived in central and northern Europe 4,500 years ago were settled farmers who grew cereals, vegetables and fruit, and crops such as flax for making linen. They kept herds of sheep, goats and cattle, and used stone and bronze to make tools and weapons. Their main concern – other than producing enough food to eat – was safety, for both themselves and their livestock. Wild animals, such as wolves, roamed the forests, while hostile tribes were always ready to attack. To defend themselves, our Bronze Age ancestors fortified their villages with walls of wood.

Wooden walls

Most of these villages were built on the shores of lakes or by rivers, often on small islands that could easily be fortified. The 20 or so rectangular houses stood on stilts to allow for seasonal flooding. The houses had walls of timber planks, and roofs of reeds with gaps at the top to allow the smoke out. Pathways of split logs ran between the houses, along which roamed goats, sheep, pigs and other animals amid the wooden racks used to dry fish, meat and animal hides. Running around the entire village was a high timber wall in which were set a few strong gates.

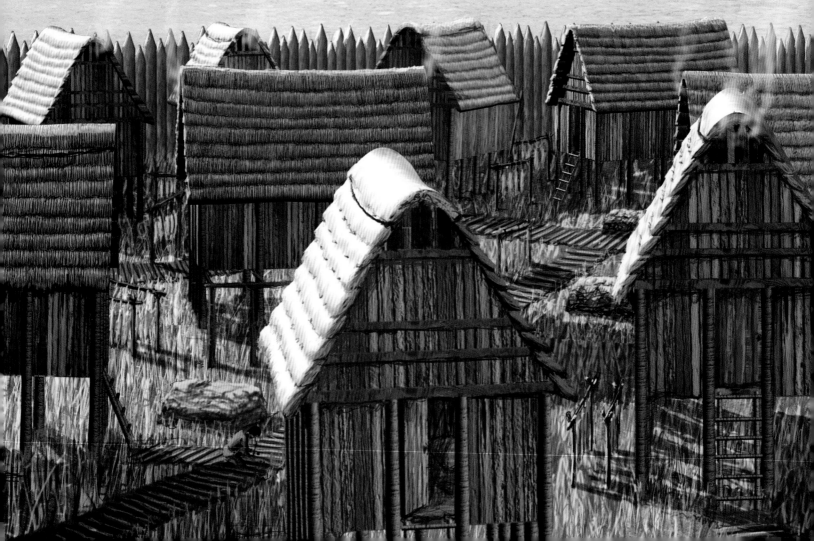

Reading the evidence

Most of these villages have now disappeared, since wood, unlike stone, does not last well over thousands of years. But in a few boggy sites that have preserved the wood, such as beside the lakes in Switzerland and Poland and along various German rivers, remains of wooden posts and evidence of wooden walls have come to light. Numerous artefacts, such as pottery jugs, bronze pins, strips of textile and stone and bronze axe heads, have also been found.

Archaeologists have been able to use these remains to piece together a picture of what life was like for our ancestors in their fortified villages by the lake.

▼ Lake houses had a life of about 40 years. After that the wooden walls and stilts that had been continuously exposed to the damp conditions of the lake became seriously decayed and eventually collapsed. The inhabitants then moved to a new site and began to construct their new village.

Maiden castle

Think of a castle or a fort, and you immediately imagine a great stone building towering over the countryside. But many early forts were built not of stone, but of the earth on which they stood, piled up into huge ramparts many metres in height. One such earthwork is Maiden castle in Dorset, southern England.

What is in a name?
Do not be fooled by the name – Maiden castle is not actually a castle but a vast hillfort. It was constructed around 300BCE by the ancient Britons on the site of an earlier Stone Age camp. The fort consisted of circular ramparts, each up to 30m tall, wrapped around the top of a hill 3.2km in circumference. The town itself covered 18ha (hectares) and contained stone and wooden houses, granaries, stores, the chief's house and other buildings, all linked together by wood and gravel tracks.

▲ Vespasian (CE9–79) was a very successful Roman military commander, taking part in the invasion of England in CE43 and the suppression of the Jewish revolt in CE66, among other campaigns. He became Roman emperor in CE69, bringing peace and prosperity to the empire until his death ten years later.

▶ Maiden castle stands on top of a broad hill commanding the countryside for kilometres around. The main entrance was guarded by a labyrinth of earthworks through which any attackers would have had to pick their way under a hail of slingshots before reaching the wooden gates into the town.

The Roman conquest

Maiden castle was therefore both a fort and a town, a place where local people were secure against enemy tribes. Around 50BCE, it became the tribal capital of the Durotriges and was one of the most prosperous towns in southern England. As such, it attracted the attention of the Romans, who invaded England in CE43. A Roman legion led by Vespasian attacked the town, massacring most of its inhabitants and destroying buildings. Those who survived were taken in captivity to the nearby new Roman town of Durnovaria, present-day Dorchester.

Beach warfare

We know much about Maiden castle because the famous British archaeologist Sir Mortimer Wheeler (1890–1977) excavated the site from 1934 to 1937. He found the graves of 34 people, their skeletons showing the wounds inflicted by Roman swords and ballista bolts. He also found 22,000 pebbles carried up from the beach some 5km away. The ancient Britons used these, ineffectually, as slingshots in the final battle against their Roman conquerors.

▲ A typical house at Maiden castle consisted of a ring of wooden posts with perhaps a central post supporting the conical roof of timber and thatch. An entire family would live together in the house, sleeping on the floor and cooking over a wood fire. A hole in the roof allowed smoke to escape.

The Great Wall of China

Most forts consist of a few buildings surrounded by a high outer wall. More than 2,000 years ago, however, the Chinese decided that individual forts, no matter how many of them they built, could not protect their country from attack, so they turned China itself into a nation-sized fort by building a great wall.

◀ In 221BCE, Zheng (259–210BCE), the leader of the northwestern Chinese state of Qin, defeated the last of his enemies and united the whole of China under a single leader for the first time. He took the title First Sovereign Qin emperor, or Qin Shi Huangdi, and gave his name – Qin is pronounced 'chin' – to the empire itself. Zheng ruled only until 210BCE, but the empire he founded lasted until its overthrow in 1912.

▲ Qin Shi Huangdi's tomb – 64km outside Xi'an in central China – is guarded by 6,000 life-sized warriors and their horses and 1,400 chariots and cavalrymen, all made of terracotta and armed with bronze weapons. The figures were individually modelled and arranged in rows in three underground chambers. They stood undiscovered for more than 2,000 years until they were unearthed in 1974.

Earthworks

The Great Wall of China began life in around 400BCE as a long series of earthen walls. It was built to mark the frontiers between the various Chinese states, and to act as a barrier to prevent the barbarian nomads of Mongolia and Manchuria sweeping south into the fertile plains of northern China. In about 214BCE, the first Chinese emperor, Qin Shi Huangdi, ordered that these walls be linked together and rebuilt into a continuous stone fortification that stretched 2,415km along the entire northern frontier of his new empire. Vast gangs of labourers were conscripted from all over China to build this wall, many of whom died during its complicated construction.

A moving wall

Over the years, the wall was strengthened and extended westwards, often along new routes, until the Ming emperors, who ruled China from 1368 to 1644, rebuilt the wall some distance to the south of the first structure. Their wall – the one we see today – is more than 4,000km long, running from the Gulf of Liaodong in the east across the mountains of northern China to the deserts of Gansu province in the west. The wall is an average of 9m tall, with an 8m-wide base sloping to a width of 6m at the top. Watchtowers along its length housed cannons and other armaments, while the broad walkway along its top allowed soldiers to move at speed in times of danger.

▼ The Great Wall of China is said to be the only man-made object visible from the moon, but since it is not much wider than an average road that is impossible! It is not unique – the Romans built a similar wall across the north of England to keep out the hostile Scots – but it is the longest man-made structure in the world.

Masada

In CE66, the Jews rose in revolt against the Roman empire. They fought a lengthy and violent guerrilla war against the occupying Roman army, which in response inflicted massive destruction throughout Judea (now part of Palestine). After the capture of the Jewish capital, Jerusalem, in CE70, a few extremists fought on, making their last and dramatic stand at the hilltop fortress of Masada.

Royal stronghold

The site of the fortress of Masada consists of a flat-topped rocky outcrop, 9.5ha in size. Masada was first fortified by the Jewish kings during the 2nd century BCE. Then, from 37 to 31BCE, it was extensively rebuilt as a palace and personal stronghold by Herod (ruled 37 to 4BCE), king of Roman-occupied Judea at the time of the birth of Christ. Herod surrounded the flat top of Masada with high walls, and inside them built two royal palaces, a synagogue, heated bathhouses and storehouses.

▼ The Roman army was the finest in the world at the time, but it was no match for the Jewish guerrilla forces. The well-armed Romans preferred to fight in open combat on the battlefield. The Jews avoided this, assaulting the Roman infantry with slingshots and javelins and retreating into the hills when attacked.

◄ In CE70, Roman troops led by Titus (CE39–81, Roman emperor from CE79 to 81), besieged and occupied Jerusalem, destroying the Jewish temple and many other buildings. The Arch of Titus in the Forum at Rome, in Italy, celebrates this victory in great detail.

▲ Much of what we know about the final stand at Masada comes from Flavius Josephus (b. CE37), a Jewish priest and governor of Galilee who supported the rebels until his capture by the Romans in CE67. He then changed sides, becoming a Roman citizen and writing histories of the Jews.

The Jewish revolt

After Herod's death in 4BCE, Roman soldiers garrisoned Masada until they withdrew at the start of the Jewish revolt in CE66. The Zealots, an extreme Jewish sect, then occupied Masada, using it as a base for their guerrilla activities against the Roman forces. When the Romans finally captured and sacked Jerusalem in CE70, the Zealots withdrew to a few well-defended fortresses. One by one, the Romans picked these off, until only Masada remained in Jewish hands.

The Roman siege

In CE72, the Roman commander Flavius Silva (Roman governor of Judea from CE71 to 81) began the siege of Masada, encircling the garrison so that none of its occupants could escape. He then constructed an earthen ramp up to the western side, on top of which he built a stone siege tower, and moved up battering rams and catapults. By spring CE73, Silva was ready to attack.

▲ Archaeologists discovered the pottery lots at Masada in 1963. They found that one belonged to Ben Ya'ir. It is possible that he was the last man alive, and that he killed himself after killing the remaining men.

Mass suicide

Inside Masada, the leader of the Zealots, Ben Ya'ir (d. CE73), made a momentous decision. He ordered the entire fortress, except the food stores, to be burned to show that they were acting out of pride, not desperation. Ya'ir then ordered the married men to slay their own families before casting lots to select ten of them to kill the rest of the garrison. The ten then cast lots again to select one of them to kill the other nine before killing himself. When the Romans broke in, they were met not by an army but by a graveyard. Masada has remained a symbol of Jewish resistance ever since.

▼ Masada stands on a rocky outcrop overlooking the Dead Sea and the Judean desert, in the southeast of what is now Israel. Its water supply came from huge underground cisterns and aqueducts cut into the solid rock, while much of its food was grown on the flat, fertile ground on the top of the outcrop.

Castel Sant'Angelo

Most castles undergo a few changes of use during their lives, evolving from a fortified stronghold into perhaps a military headquarters and then a private residence. But none has undergone such a dramatic transformation as the Castel Sant'Angelo – the Castle of the Holy Angel – in Rome, in Italy, which began life not as a castle, but as a tomb!

▲ Successive popes from 1390 onwards turned the castle into a luxurious papal palace, commissioning the most famous artists and sculptors of the day to decorate the many papal private apartments, chapels and state rooms. Pope Clement VII (in office from 1523 to 1534) hired Giovanni da Udine (1487–1535) to paint the elaborate frescoes in this bathroom.

The imperial tomb

In CE123, the Roman emperor Hadrian (ruled CE117 to 138) decided to build an impressive mausoleum (tomb) next to the banks of the River Tiber in Rome. He designed the building himself, based on an earlier magnificent tomb built for Emperor Augustus (ruled 27BCE to CE14) a century earlier. The mausoleum consisted of a square plinth 86.3m long. On top of this was set a cylindrical structure 64m in diameter and covered on top with earth and planted with cypress trees. A small round building sat at the very top. Hadrian's tomb and rooms for future burials were in the centre of the mausoleum, linked by a long gallery to an entrance on the riverbank. Ivory-coloured marble covered the whole structure, which was adorned with numerous statues.

◄ Roman soldiers successfully protected the mausoleum from attack until the Roman empire itself fell in CE476. In CE537, however, an Ostrogoth army from northern Italy besieged it. Roman defenders broke up Castel Sant'Angelo's many marble statues and used their heads, arms and legs as ammunition to hurl down on top of their attackers.

Divine intervention

For almost a century, the mausoleum received the imperial bodies, but by CE275 it had become part of the massive walls built to protect Rome from attack. By CE500, it was used as a prison.

On 29 August CE590, Pope Gregory I (in office from CE590 to 614) led a procession through Rome asking God to rid the city of plague. When the people approached the mausoleum, the skies darkened and a rainbow-like figure of an archangel appeared overhead. The plague lifted, and from then on the mausoleum became known as the Castle of the Holy Angel.

Papal palace

Over the next 1,000 years, the castle played an important part in the turbulent history of Rome, serving both as a fortress and as a place of refuge for successive popes. In 1277, a fortified walkway was built from the Vatican to allow popes quick access to the castle in times of danger. After it was severely damaged by an uprising in 1387, Pope Boniface IX (in office from 1389 to 1404) began work in 1390 to turn the castle into a papal palace. In 1870, the castle was used as a barracks and military prison before becoming the museum it is today.

▲ In 1527, the mercenary army of the Holy Roman emperor Charles V (ruled 1519 to 1556) mutinied against their commanders. They sacked Rome in an attempt to enrich themselves, looting its fine buildings and killing at least 30,000 people. Pope Clement VII fled to Castel Sant'Angelo, where he was besieged for six months before reaching agreement with Charles V.

▼ During the 17th century CE, the bridge connecting the mausoleum with the other bank of the Tiber was decorated with ten statues of angels by the famous sculptor Gianlorenzo Bernini (1598–1680), giving it the name Ponte Sant'Angelo (Holy Angel's Bridge).

Ait Benhaddou

The ksar (fortified village) of Ait Benhaddou might look familiar to you, even if you have never been to eastern Morocco, in Africa, to see it for yourself. But look closely at films such as *Lawrence of Arabia*, and there is the village and its surrounding landscape on screen, for this stark but beautiful land has featured in many Hollywood films.

▲ The Berbers are skilled craftworkers, producing beautiful handicrafts. Even their swords and scabbards are ornate, made of beaten silver and then inlaid with other metals and precious gems.

People on the move

Morocco has had a complex history, as successive waves of Phoenician, Carthaginian, Roman, Vandal, Arab, Saharan, Spanish and French traders and conquerors have stamped their mark on the country. As a result, the Berbers and other Moroccan tribes were pushed into the remote mountainous regions. Many of them fortified their villages to protect themselves against these and other hostile forces.

Safe trade

Ait Benhaddou stands on the historic trade route from the Moroccan city of Marrakech south across the Sahara desert to the great trading post of Timbuktu. It was built by the Berbers, although no-one is sure of the exact date, and it has since been added to many times. Like every ksar, it is protected by an impressive set of walls and towers.

Magical colours

The merchants of Ait Benhaddou grew wealthy from trade, building a number of impressive kasbahs (castles) to protect themselves and their animals. The other villagers lived in small houses packed together on the hillside, using the igherm (communal granary) to store their grain. All these buildings were made from sun-baked bricks of earth mixed with water and straw. For its beauty, and its history, Ait Benhaddou is now one of UNESCO's World Heritage Sites.

▶ Most Moroccan medinas (towns) such as Taroudant (right) are enclosed by high walls, with numerous look-out towers along their length. Gates into the medina are heavily fortified.

▼ The Berbers and other Moroccans are renowned for their riding skills. Displays of horsemanship known as fantasias are performed according to strict rules. The riders gallop very fast, holding their guns in the air. At a signal from the leader, they fire in unison.

SUMMARY OF CHAPTER 1: THE FIRST FORTS

Fort or castle?

You will already have realized that the difference between a fort and a castle (and a fortress and a fortification) is not very clear. Maiden castle might sound as if it should have had stone walls and battlements – just like a medieval castle – but it was in fact a large hillfort made of earth; while the fortress of Masada had high walls around it and was used as a residence, just like a castle.

In reality, the words are often interchangeable. A castle is technically a large fortified building or set of buildings, while a fort is a fortified enclosure with buildings inside it. A fortification (or fort for short!) is a defensive structure such as an earthwork, wall or tower, and a fortress is a large fort. But do not be confused, since all of these definitions imply a military structure of one form

Rillaton gold cup, c. 2000BCE (early Bronze Age artefact)

or another, even if their owners or keepers are not very clear when it comes to deciding whether they want their structures to be known as castles or forts.

Where in the world?

The forts and castles in this chapter range from fortified lake settlements in northern Europe to converted mausoleums in Rome; and ksars or fortified villages in Morocco. We could have visited many other ancient forts and castles in almost every continent in the world, with the exception of Australasia, where the Aboriginal peoples had no need to build permanent structures at this time.

What all these castles and forts have in common is that they were built by people with a need to defend themselves and their livestock from attack. All of them take advantage of natural features, such as hilltops or lakes, and many of them also command major trading routes or dominate important cities. It takes walls and ramparts to create a fort or castle, but most importantly it also requires a good location to make sure that it is as secure as possible.

Go further...

Dig out more information about archaeology:
www.digonsite.com/

Explore Maiden castle and other English Heritage sites:
www.english-heritage.org.uk

Learn more about the Great Wall of China:
www.enchantedlearning.com/subjects/greatwall/

For more information on Masada:
http://mosaic.lk.net/g-masada.html

Awesome Archaeology by Nick Arnold (Scholastic, 2001)

Eyewitness Archaeology by Jane McIntosh (Dorling Kindersley, 1994)

Archaeologist
Studies the remains of ancient forts.

Conservationist
Preserves ancient remains.

Tour guide
Escorts visitors around historic sites.

Computer graphic artist
Recreates ancient sites on screen.

Illustrator or **photographer**
Documents the ancient sites.

Historian
Writes about ancient forts and castles.

Surveyor
Maps ancient sites.

Visit Maiden castle (c. 300BCE), an ancient British hillfort.
www.english-heritage.org.uk/

Explore Navan fort (Emain Macha), a c. 3rd-century BCE Celtic Iron Age fort in Co Armagh, Ireland.
www.goireland.com

Hadrian's Wall – an early 2nd-century CE Roman wall – runs through Cumbria, Northumberland and Tyne and Wear, in England.
www.hadrians-wall.org/
e-mail: info@hadrians-wall.org

Explore a 9th-century CE Scottish defensive tower in Abernethy, Perth and Kinross.
www.visitscotland.com/

CHAPTER 2

The great age of castles

Starting in the 9th century CE, local rulers began to build castles to defend themselves and their families from attack by their enemies. These castles were first built of wood and then replaced later with far more complex structures of stone and brick. Towering above the countryside, castles were often the biggest and most impressive buildings in the area.

They served as homes and fortresses, headquarters and prisons, and incorporated the latest thinking in building design, construction, engineering and military technology. For more than 800 years, these castles and their owners dominated the political, military and geographical landscape, not just in Europe, but as far afield as India, Japan, the Middle East and South America.

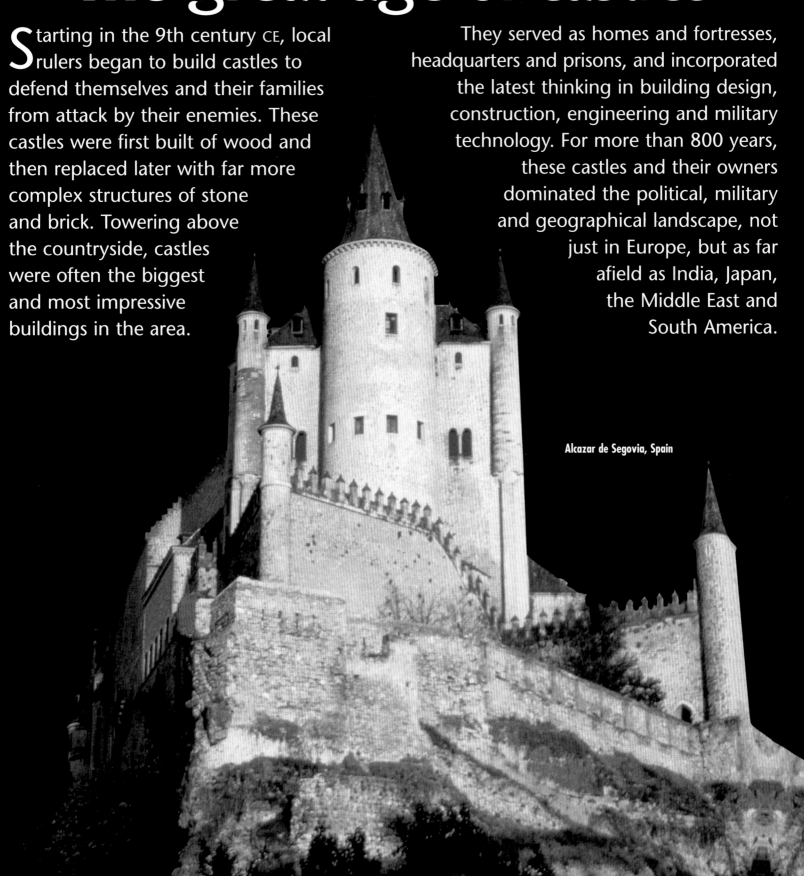

Alcazar de Segovia, Spain

Motte and bailey castles

motte
drawbridge
bailey

In western Europe, the first castles appeared in the 9th and 10th centuries CE, a time of great lawlessness. Local lords built simple wooden ringworks (enclosures) on top of earthen ramparts, which were surrounded by ditches, to protect themselves and their families from invaders. These simple structures ushered in a period of castle building that was to last for nearly 800 years.

▲ The first castles to be built in western Europe consisted of a simple fortified bailey with a bridge up to a protected motte or mound. Simple and quick to build, these castles were very effective at defending their occupants.

▼ The Bayeux Tapestry records the building (below) at Hastings, southern England, of a motte, a week or so before the great battle on 14 October 1066 at which William of Normandy won the English crown. The workers were probably local Saxons forced into service by the Norman army. A finished motte castle (right) is shown later in the tapestry.

The Norman invasion

The first castles were built to protect their inhabitants from attack, as well as to provide a safe garrison for local soldiers. But by the 11th century CE, castles were mainly used as bases from which to subdue the local peasants. The reason for this great change was the 1066 conquest of England by William of Normandy. Faced with a hostile Saxon population, King William needed to assert his authority over his new kingdom.

The motte and bailey

William brought with him a design for a castle he had developed in Normandy. This consisted of a wooden-fenced bailey (courtyard), surrounded by a moat and protected by an earthen rampart. Within the bailey were stables, workshops, the well and perhaps even a chapel. Separated from the bailey by its own moat was the motte – a mound of pressed layers of soil at least 5m high – on which stood a wooden tower and lookout post. Access to the motte was by drawbridge.

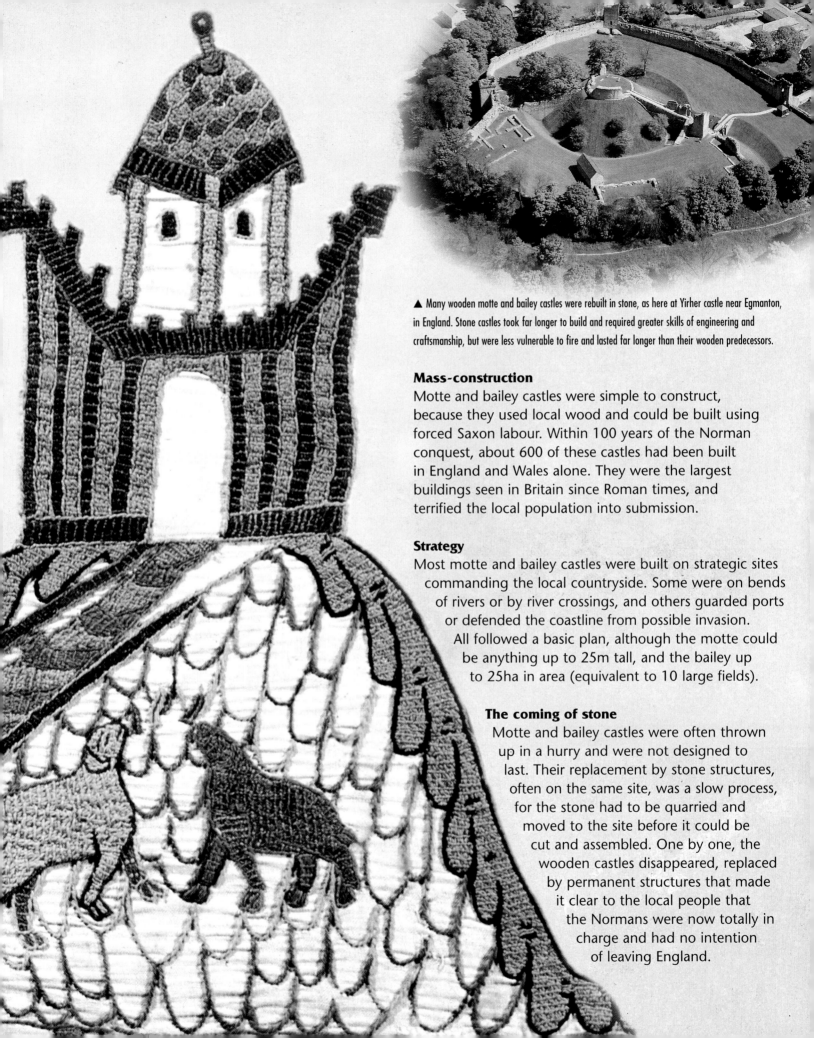

▲ Many wooden motte and bailey castles were rebuilt in stone, as here at Yirher castle near Egmanton, in England. Stone castles took far longer to build and required greater skills of engineering and craftsmanship, but were less vulnerable to fire and lasted far longer than their wooden predecessors.

Mass-construction

Motte and bailey castles were simple to construct, because they used local wood and could be built using forced Saxon labour. Within 100 years of the Norman conquest, about 600 of these castles had been built in England and Wales alone. They were the largest buildings seen in Britain since Roman times, and terrified the local population into submission.

Strategy

Most motte and bailey castles were built on strategic sites commanding the local countryside. Some were on bends of rivers or by river crossings, and others guarded ports or defended the coastline from possible invasion. All followed a basic plan, although the motte could be anything up to 25m tall, and the bailey up to 25ha in area (equivalent to 10 large fields).

The coming of stone

Motte and bailey castles were often thrown up in a hurry and were not designed to last. Their replacement by stone structures, often on the same site, was a slow process, for the stone had to be quarried and moved to the site before it could be cut and assembled. One by one, the wooden castles disappeared, replaced by permanent structures that made it clear to the local people that the Normans were now totally in charge and had no intention of leaving England.

Building in stone

The first stone castles appeared in western Europe during the 10th century CE. Over the next 600 years, these massive structures dominated the countryside, acting as the headquarters of the local lord, a garrison for his army, a house for his family and a prison for his opponents.

The appearance of stone

The first stone castles were constructed in the late 10th century CE, at either Langeais or Doué-la-Fontaine in western France – historians are unsure which one came first. Many more were built after the Norman invasion of England in 1066, as permanent stone structures replaced the wooden motte and bailey castles (see pages 22–23) quickly erected after the invasion. Among these were Chepstow (c. 1067) on the border of England and Wales, the Tower of London (work began on the stone White Tower in 1078) and the vast castle of Rochester (c. late 1060s), guarding the strategic River Medway crossing on the road between the English Channel and London.

▶ Castle windows were not designed for letting in light, let alone for looking at the view! Technically known as arrow loops, their function was purely to allow an archer to fire his arrow or crossbow at the enemy without being hit by the return fire. The only windows with glass would have been in the chapel.

Spiral staircases revolved in either direction, but most went up clockwise (like this one at Rochester), allowing a defending soldier to fight with his sword in his right hand while retreating up the steps. Some spiral staircases rose from the ground floor straight up to the roof, with a hidden staircase giving access to the floors in between. These staircases, and other defensive devices, were designed to confuse an intruder.

The great tower

At first stone castles consisted of a single great donjon (tower), often known as a keep. These towers could be any shape – square, rectangular or round – and had massive, stone walls, narrow slits for windows, and a single entrance often raised up above the ground and approached by an exterior staircase. The tower contained both living quarters for the lord and his family, and lodgings for his soldiers. Later, curtain walls were built around the tower, creating a large bailey where animals could be kept and horses stabled. Fortified gatehouses, often including a portcullis, protected the entrance, while a drawbridge over the moat provided extra defence for those inside the walls.

Slow work

Each castle was built to its own design, and varied from place to place, according to the wealth and needs of its owner and the quality of the local stone. Building was a slow process: on average, a tower rose 3m per year. As the stone was quarried, an army of labourers transported it to the site, which had already been cleared. Skilled masons then cut and placed the stone. Once built, many castles were whitewashed – the White Tower of London gets its name from the whitewash applied during the 13th century CE – while others were coated in plaster. The cost of construction was huge; historians estimate that up to ten per cent of the English national budget from 1155 to 1215 went on castle building.

Château Gaillard

The impressive fortress of Château Gaillard stands on a loop of land sticking out into the River Seine, in northern France. It was constructed between 1195 and 1198 by one of the most famous kings in medieval Europe, Richard I, king of England, and was supposed to be impregnable. By 1204, however, it had fallen to the troops of his fiercest enemy, Philip II of France.

England in France

As king of England, Richard I (ruled 1189 to 1199) had inherited huge estates in northern and western France. But most of Richard's French possessions were also claimed by the French kings, who resented the huge power the English had in France. Richard I decided to build Château Gaillard to protect his frontier from French invasions.

▲ Richard I was king for ten years, but he only spent seven months in England. The rest of the time he fought in Crusades in the Holy Land (see pages 30–31) or tried to protect his French empire from Philip II. He was renowned for his bravery and nicknamed 'Coeur de Lion' – the Lionheart.

▼ At the centre of Château Gaillard was the great keep, with walls more than 2.5m thick. The fortress had three courtyards and was protected by three massive stone walls, each up to 9m high. A huge moat surrounded the outer walls.

Belfry, a mobile siege tower made of wood

Traction trébuchet to hurl rocks and other missiles

Walls of butter!

The English king built his castle on a spur of rock 90m above the Seine to dominate the surrounding countryside. He boasted he could hold his castle "even if the walls were made of butter". But he died before his claim could be put to the test, and his brother John became king.

The siege

Philip II first attacked Château Gaillard in 1203, soon encircling the castle itself. The English commander, Roger de Lacy, drove out all the women, children and elderly from the castle in order to save his food stocks for the soldiers. But Philip II refused to accept them, forcing them all to spend the winter shivering and hungry near the castle moat until he eventually relented.

In spring 1204, the siege began in earnest. The French hauled up catapults and a belfry, and began to fill in the castle moat so that they could approach the outer walls on level ground. Protected by mantlets – large wooden shields – sappers (miners) began to undermine one of the outer towers. According to one contemporary source, the tower came tumbling down.

▲ After the siege, Château Gaillard was repaired by its new owners until, in 1603, Henry IV (ruled 1589 to 1610) ordered that its defensive walls be dismantled. Over the years, the stone was taken away and used in the construction of various local buildings, leaving the castle in the ruined state we see today.

Victory

The French rushed into the outer courtyard and discovered an unguarded latrine shaft, which gave them easy, if smelly, access up through the walls to the middle courtyard. Here, they drew up a trébuchet and began to attack the thinner, innermost walls. Sappers set to work, and these walls too came tumbling down. As the French stormed in, the English garrison surrendered and the 140 defenders were taken prisoner. Château Gaillard was now in French hands.

Spring-loaded catapult to hurl flaming missiles and rocks

Concentric castles

During the second half of the 13th century CE, a new type of castle appeared in western Europe, many of them built by Edward I of England. The concentric castle, with its double ring of defensive walls and other groundbreaking features such as a reinforced gatehouse, was based on an old design, but it proved remarkably effective in keeping out attackers.

▲ Edward I, who ruled England from 1272 to 1307, was nicknamed 'Hammer of the Scots', after his attempt to unite the kingdoms of England and Scotland.

The need for change

The first stone castles had been constructed with a single outer wall. This was strong and tall, but vulnerable to siege engines and mining works. Once the wall was undermined or fell down, the siege was effectively over and the castle easily occupied. A better system of defence was required to make a castle truly impregnable.

▼ The first concentric castle to be built in Britain, Caerphilly castle, was constructed between 1268 and 1271 by Gilbert de Clare (1243–1295) – the most powerful English baron in south Wales – during his campaign against the Welsh prince, Llywelyn ap Gruffydd (ruled 1246 to 1282).

Inspiration from the east

The solution to this problem came from an unlikely source – the ancient walls of Constantinople, in Turkey, built by Emperor Theodosius II between CE 410 and 447. In order to protect the eastern capital of the Roman empire, Theodosius encircled the city with two sets of walls only 4.6m apart. The inner walls were about 9m tall, the outer 4.6m. Both walls had massive protruding towers along their length at regular intervals. In front of these walls was a deep moat, bridged only by the five main entrances to the city. From the time of their construction to the arrival of the crusaders in 1204, these walls had never been breached.

A winning design

It was the crusaders who carried back this new design to western Europe, as well as using it to design their own castles, notably Krak des Chevaliers (see pages 30–31), in the Biblical Holy Land of what is now Israel and Palestine. The concentric design proved very effective, since defenders on the high inner walls could fire over the heads of their fellow defenders on the lower outer walls without, in theory, harming them.

If required, the defenders on the outer walls could also rush out to attack the besieging enemy, confident that the castle remained well-defended from its inner walls. Cylindrical towers stood at each corner of the inner walls, while access to the castle was limited to one or two heavily fortified twin-towered gatehouses. The overall design varied from site to site, but many of these new castles were regular in shape, and some almost perfectly square.

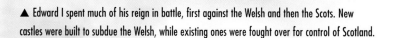

▲ Edward I spent much of his reign in battle, first against the Welsh and then the Scots. New castles were built to subdue the Welsh, while existing ones were fought over for control of Scotland.

Concentric castles soon sprouted up across Europe. Existing castles were given new outer sets of walls, while ten new castles were built by Edward I in north Wales to subdue the principality after its conquest in 1282. This vast programme of castle building involved 150 masons and 400 carpenters, as well as 1,000 diggers and 8,000 woodcutters to clear the land before construction began. Many towns, such as Carcassonne (see pages 36–37) in France, were also fortified by concentric walls.

▼ This aerial view of Caerphilly castle, in Wales, clearly shows its concentric design, strong gatehouses and surrounding moat. These features made it the strongest castle in the south of the principality.

◄ Concentric castles were not just built in Britain. Muiderslot in the Netherlands – 'slot' means castle in Dutch – was built around 1280s and clearly shows the influence of King Edward's Welsh castles.

Krak des Chevaliers

In 1095, Pope Urban II (in office from 1088 to 1099), head of the Christian church in western Europe, issued a call to arms. The Muslim Seljuk Turks, who controlled the Biblical Holy Land of what is now Israel and Palestine, were preventing pilgrims travelling from Europe to holy sites such as Jerusalem. The pope promised spiritual benefits to those who would fight to reclaim the land from the Muslims. Thousands of crusaders from many countries answered his call and travelled to the Holy Land. There they built a series of castles, including Krak des Chevaliers.

▲ During the final siege in 1270, siege engines caused great damage to the outer walls and towers. Catapults hurled huge missiles against the stonework to weaken the structure, while trébuchets launched burning balls of tar and straw to set light to interior woodwork.

Copying the enemy

Krak des Chevaliers, in what is now western Syria, was a Muslim fortress until captured in 1099 by the crusaders. In 1144, the Crusader ruler of the area gave the fortress to the Knights Hospitallers, a religious order of knights, who turned it into the vast and impressive castle we see today.

Krak des Chevaliers – the Castle of Knights – stands above the west bank of the River Orontes, from where it could command the strategic north to south route from Syria to the Holy Land. The castle could only be approached from one direction, making it almost impregnable. But the Knights Hospitallers took no chances when rebuilding Krak des Chevaliers. They copied many of the Muslim fortifications they had encountered on crusade.

▼ The Crusades lasted from 1095 to 1291, when the final Christian stronghold in the region, Acre, fell to the Muslims. Thousands of knights from all over Europe sailed to the Holy Land, or took the more dangerous route overland through Turkey. Despite this huge endeavour, the crusaders failed to dislodge the Muslims from the Holy Land.

Building for strength

The basic plan of the castle was concentric (see pages 28–29), but the Hospitallers added many extra features. The inner wall consisted of huge, interconnected towers overlooking a moat, which served as a reservoir to supply water to the knights. The outer wall, added in the early 1200s, included several semi-circular towers which could deflect any missiles fired at them by siege engines.

A crucial weakness

Despite its huge strength, Krak des Chevaliers had one major weakness. All the water in the castle flowed into it from the surrounding hills along an aqueduct. If the aqueduct was blocked, the castle would run out of water, a serious problem in such a hot region.

◀ The first Hospitallers founded a hospital in Jerusalem in around 1070, to care for sick pilgrims. When the city fell to the crusaders in 1099, they were recognized as a formal military, religious and medical order of knights known as the Knights Hospitallers of St John of Jerusalem.

▶ Krak des Chevaliers was more than just a castle. It was also the headquarters of the Knights Hospitallers, whose commander occupied a room high up in one of the towers of the inner wall. Here, he planned with his fellow knights how best to defend the castle.

Siege after siege

Krak des Chevaliers was repeatedly besieged by Muslim forces. The great warrior Saladin (1138–1193) failed to conquer it in 1188, as did his successors. But in 1270, an Egyptian army, led by Sultan Baybars (ruled 1260 to 1277), surrounded the castle and cut off its water supply. The 200 knights inside the castle held out for six weeks, but Baybars' siege engines caused serious damage to the outer walls, allowing his forces to enter the castle. The Hospitallers surrendered on favourable terms and were allowed to leave the castle alive. Krak des Chevaliers was finally captured.

Riverbank castles

Sail on the River Rhine today, particularly the stretch between Mainz and Köln in Germany, and you are immediately struck by the large number of castles on both riverbanks. Yet few of these impressive buildings started life as castles, most having the far less exciting role of collecting tolls (taxes) from passing ships.

▲ In Poland, stone replaced wood as the main building material for castles much later than in the rest of western Europe, because wood was the most readily available building material. The original wooden Bedzin castle (above), in Poland, was twice destroyed by fire before Casimir the Great (ruled 1333 to 1370) finally rebuilt it in stone.

Robber Barons

In the Middle Ages, the Rhine was not the peaceful river it is today. Rival German kings and princes fought for control of the river and its lucrative trade. They built castles along the banks to control the flow of people and goods, and introduced very high tolls which they used to enrich themselves and their families. Some of these princes were known as Robber Barons, since their tolls were so high.

The Robber Barons acquired such great power that the main trading cities on the river – which were badly affected by the high tolls they had to pay to ship goods from one city to another – formed the League of Rhenish Cities in 1254 to challenge them. In 1272, the German emperor, Rudolf I (Holy Roman emperor from 1273 to 1291), came to the cities' aid and crushed the barons for good. Four of their castles were captured, others weakened, and gradually peace was restored.

The toll tower

Local rulers still needed to collect tolls, however. One such was Louis the Bavarian (Holy Roman emperor from 1314 to 1346) whose family held extensive lands in the Rhine valley. In 1327, Louis built a five-sided tower – the Pfalzgrafenstein – on a small islet in the Rhine, from which his ships could row or sail out into the river and intercept any passing craft. They collected any tolls due and made sure the river was not being used for hostile purposes.

▲ Louis the Bavarian, here seen in a more saintly guise, built Pfalzgrafenstein to collect river dues and to assert his control over a stretch of the River Rhine.

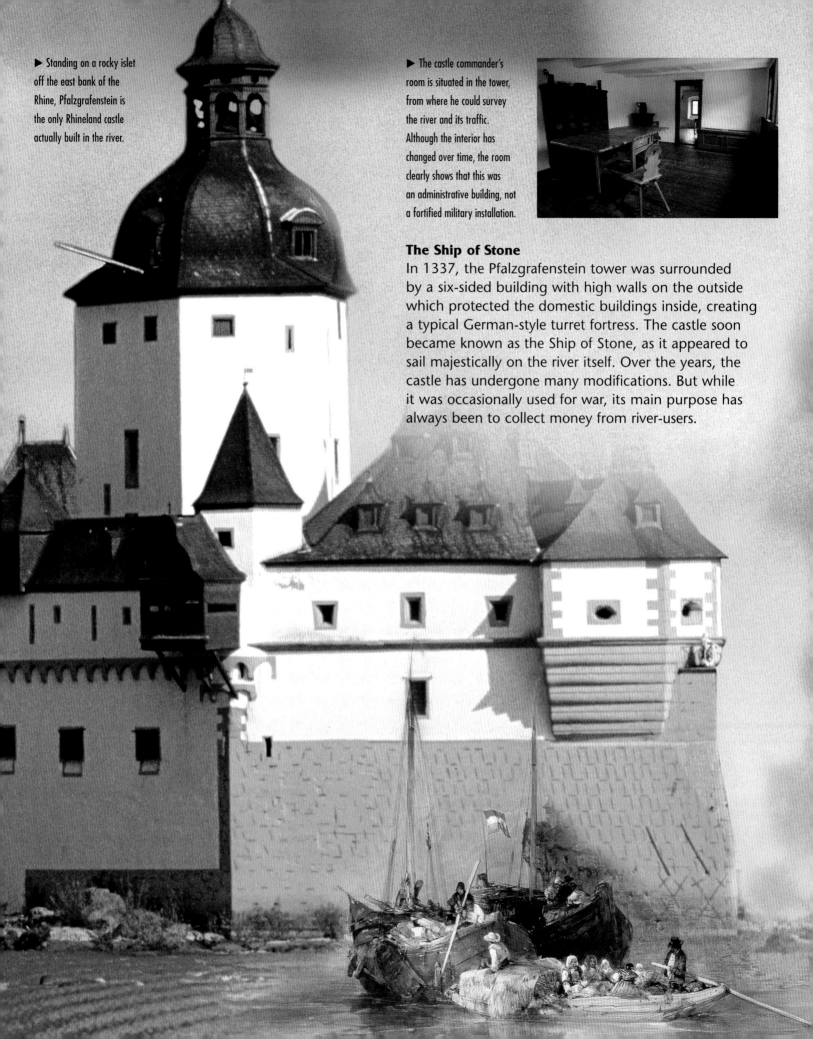

▶ Standing on a rocky islet off the east bank of the Rhine, Pfalzgrafenstein is the only Rhineland castle actually built in the river.

▶ The castle commander's room is situated in the tower, from where he could survey the river and its traffic. Although the interior has changed over time, the room clearly shows that this was an administrative building, not a fortified military installation.

The Ship of Stone

In 1337, the Pfalzgrafenstein tower was surrounded by a six-sided building with high walls on the outside which protected the domestic buildings inside, creating a typical German-style turret fortress. The castle soon became known as the Ship of Stone, as it appeared to sail majestically on the river itself. Over the years, the castle has undergone many modifications. But while it was occasionally used for war, its main purpose has always been to collect money from river-users.

The Alhambra of Granada

Think of a castle or fortress, and you picture a forbidding building with huge, stone walls, little decoration and even less in the way of comfort or luxury. In most cases this is true, but in the south of Spain there is a remarkable fortress that is more like a villa with beautiful gardens.

A beautiful fort

The Alhambra of Granada was built between 1238 and 1358 by the Moors – Muslim Arabs from northwest Africa who invaded and conquered most of Spain in CE711. The Moors were skilled fighters who needed a secure fortress from which to control their southern Spanish kingdom, but they were also a highly cultured people, who valued fine architecture, beautiful design and luxurious living.

▼ Inside the Alhambra are many formal gardens, awash with cooling water and lush greenery. The Patio de la Acequia forms part of the Generalife, or summer palace, in the grounds of the main palace.

Built for protection

The name Alhambra comes from the Arabic word for red, the colour of the sun-dried bricks of the outer walls. The fortress stands on top of a hill, and its outer walls, with their 23 towers and four gateways, were built for defence. Inside, however, the buildings served many different functions. There were mosques for worship, seven palaces for the Moorish princes to live in, a fortress for the soldiers, a prison and even a royal mint. These were set among lush, water-filled gardens and connected to each other by covered walkways, all designed to keep the palace cool and shady in the hot summer months.

A tragic palace

Despite its beauty, the Alhambra was also a violent place. The ornate Hall of Abencerrajes got its name after one of the Moorish princes beheaded all the abencerrajes (sons of his first wife) so that his son by his second wife could succeed him. The Moors were expelled from their palace in 1492, when the Catholic kings of Spain, Ferdinand and Isabella – joint rulers who united the country by their marriage – finally drove them out of Spain. The Moors' legacy is one of the most beautiful buildings in the world.

▲ Water is carried to the Alhambra along a 1.6km-long covered watercourse from the nearby hills. Once inside the building, it supplies the numerous fountains, pools, basins and water channels that decorate the interior and its many courtyards.

▶ The rows of stone columns and arched windows of the Alhambra are all intricately decorated with geometric patterns. The decoration is made of plaster, which was applied to the stone and then engraved while still wet. Elsewhere, mosaic tiles add further decoration to the floors and lower walls.

◀ This aerial view of Carcassonne gives
an excellent idea of the extent and
complexity of its fortifications. Sitting
on top of a hill, its concentric walls,
heavily fortified citadel and massive
barbican (seen in the centre foreground)
made the city almost impregnable.

The great walled fortress towns of Europe

Ever since the first large towns and cities were built some 6,000 years ago in the Middle East, urban inhabitants have always protected themselves with defensive walls. These defences developed into state-of-the-art fortifications during the Middle Ages, particularly in western Europe.

The need for walls

Europe during the Middle Ages was a far more riotous place than it is today. Real power often lay with the king's feudal lords, who held great lands of their own and commanded private armies. Rivalry between these lords often broke out into warfare, which meant towns had to protect themselves in case they were attacked by enemy forces. A strong wall around a town or city also kept its inhabitants safe at night.

New defences

Many towns made use of existing Roman fortifications, adding to or strengthening them as required. As a further safeguard, a fortified citadel was often built into the walls to house the garrison and town's administration, while a second set of walls was built around the first to provide a double line of defence. Towers were built at regular intervals along the walls, both as lookouts and as platforms from which to fire down arrows and missiles. Entrance to the town was controlled through a highly secure barbican (gatehouse) fortification.

▲ Carcassonne is surrounded by a set of concentric walls, with 17 towers on the lower, outer wall and 29 towers on the higher, inner wall.

Carcassonne

Carcassonne, in southern France, is probably the best-defended town of this type. Traditionally ruled by the Trencavel family, the town became a royal fortress in 1209, but was besieged in 1240 when the Trencavels tried to recapture it from the king, Louis IX (ruled 1226 to 1270). At this point, it still had many of its original Roman and Visigoth walls, and was in places more than 1,300 years old. Louis IX therefore decided to rebuild the town to make it impregnable, and to safeguard his southern border with Spain.

▶ Monteriggioni in Tuscany, in Italy, is one of the most perfect walled towns in Europe. It was built in 1214, with a single almost circular wall, 560m long and punctuated by 14 towers. The town is laid out either side of a single street.

France's most fortified town

Once he had moved all the inhabitants into a new town across the River Aube, Louis IX strengthened and raised the existing walls and surrounded them with a second set of fortifications. New towers and barbicans were constructed and other fortifications strengthened. By the time the work was completed in 1285, the town had acquired a reputation as the most heavily fortified town in France. No-one attempted to besiege or capture it, and it maintained its formidable reputation for centuries, until the nearby border with Spain was pushed further south during the 17th century CE.

▼ The Romans first fortified the hilltop of Carcassonne during the 1st century BCE. Some of their walls were later used by the Visigoths during the 6th century CE as the basis of their own fortifications, which protected the town for more than 700 years.

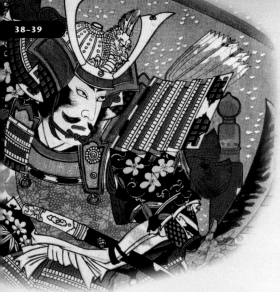

Himeji castle

Towering above the Harima plain of central Japan, the imposing wooden fortress of Himeji was built to withstand every bullet or arrow an enemy could fire at it. Yet ironically, it never saw a shot fired in anger, and soon became a palatial residence for the local daimio (lord).

The first castle

▲ The Japanese samurai was a trained warrior who fought for his daimio and was in turn served by local peasants. The daimio and their samurai held immense local power in Japan until a strong central government took control in the early 1600s.

During the Middle Ages, Japan was a largely lawless country with rival daimios fighting each other for power and influence. In 1580, one such daimio, Hashiba Hideyoshi (1536–1598), decided to build a castle at Himeji in order to strengthen his hold on the local area. At first the castle consisted only of a simple three-storey fortified tower called a tenshukaku, but by 1609 the new daimio, Ikeda Terumasa (1564–1613), had added many other buildings and fortifications to it, creating today's magnificent structure.

▲ The outer corridors of Himeji stored muskets and lances ready for use. The double rows of pegs were used as gun racks while fire beaters hung on the hooks near the ceiling.

Fortifying the castle

Himeji castle is surrounded by a moat, one arm of which tucks in behind the other to form a double barrier. Lining the inside of the moat are high walls and fortified gatehouses, protecting the outer courtyards. A series of stepped fortifications and further gatehouses protect the network of inner courtyards. At the heart of this complex stands the main eight-storey keep of Himeji, linked by lower buildings to three smaller keeps. The building's wooden frame rests on stone so it will 'bounce' if there is an earthquake, a common occurrence in Japan.

▶ Himeji castle has been nicknamed 'White Heron castle', because its curved roofs and white plastered walls reminded people of the bird often seen in Japan.

The main keep

The main keep was designed to be impregnable. It stands on a raised plinth of rock and earth and is coated with fireproof, bullet-proof white plaster to protect its wooden framework. To enter this fortress, invaders had to rush through a series of fortified entrances and twisting, narrow passages. Inside the keep, the defenders were well-prepared. Hidden openings under the roofs allowed them to drop rocks, hot oil and boiling water onto the enemy. The gunports were tilted downwards to get the best angle of fire.

▲ The Japanese believed that the larger and more elaborate the roof and gables, the greater the power and prestige of the owner of the building. At Himeji, the roofs of the castle are a riot of decoration and detail, with highly decorated gables, massive overhangs and ornate wooden shingle tiles.

Out of date

Himeji castle was built at a time when small firearms, such as handguns and muskets, were first introduced into Japan. Cannons were rare, which meant a well-designed, well-defended castle such as Himeji could have withstood almost any siege. However, the castle was also built just as the period of political instability in Japan was coming to an end. In the early 1600s, the great shogun (warlord) Ieyasu Tokugawa (1524–1616) broke the control of the powerful daimios and their samurai supporters and introduced a period of prolonged peace to the country. Himeji was redundant, and became a luxurious residence instead.

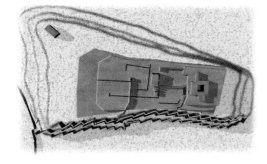

▲ The Inca capital Cuzco was built to a rigid grid pattern, with the fortress of Sacsahuaman to its west (top left of this plan).

Sacsahuaman

When the Spanish conqueror Francisco Pizarro arrived in the Inca empire of South America in 1532, he hoped to find gold and silver. He found those in abundance, but what he also discovered was one of the most awe-inspiring buildings in the entire world – the stone-built fortress of Sacsahuaman.

The Incas

The Inca empire expansion began in the 1430s and soon stretched along 3,200km of the Pacific coast of South America, from modern-day Ecuador in the north down through Peru and Bolivia to Chile in the south. The Incas created one of the most technologically advanced civilizations in the world. They built a massive road network, constructed suspension bridges to cross the many river gorges in their mountainous empire, and terraced and irrigated the steep hillsides for agriculture. Above all, they built fabulous cities and palaces, protecting them with impressive fortresses such as Sacsahuaman.

▼ The Incas never discovered the wheel, so they had to drag the locally quarried stones onto site using rollers and manual labour. They then used pulleys and ramps to raise them up into position. Each stone was individually cut and shaped so that it fitted exactly into place.

Impressive stones

Sacsahuaman – an Inca word meaning 'satisfied falcon' – was built in the mid-1400s to defend Cuzco, the Inca capital. The fortress was more than 530m long and consisted of three massive terraced walls, in places rising to more than 20m and built in a zigzag fashion to deter attacking forces. Inside these walls were three massive towers, the largest of which had a 21m-long rectangular base and rose up five storeys. The fortress easily housed 5,000 soldiers. In times of crisis, the entire population of Cuzco could retreat inside its walls.

The Incas were master stonemasons. To build Sacsahuaman they first created a small-scale model in clay. They then cut, finished and individually shaped, each stone using bronze and stone chisels and hammers and sand abrasives. The Incas were so skilled that each stone fitted exactly into place so that not even a thin blade could be inserted around it. Some of the stones at Sacsahuaman are massive – the largest still on site is 115m³ and weighs more than 360t (tonnes).

The end of empire

Despite its size and strength, the Inca empire was no match for the Spanish. In May 1532, Pizarro and his small army of 240 men and 62 horses invaded the empire. They took advantage of a civil war to quickly capture and kill the Inca emperor, Atahualpa (d.1533). Pizarro seized Cuzco in November 1533, but the Incas retreated inside Sacsahuaman. Three years later, after a bloody battle, the Spanish broke the siege and finally captured Sacsahuaman. Over the next 20 years they deliberately dismantled the fortress, so that, by 1560, little of it survived.

▶ Francisco Pizarro (1475–1541) was a Spanish explorer who led expeditions along the Pacific coast of South America. In 1532, he and his small army invaded and conquered the vast Inca empire.

Golconda

Stand in the domed entrance to Golconda fort and clap your hands, and the noise you make can be heard clearly at the highest point of the fort almost 1km away. This is no accident of acoustics but an ingenious security system designed to alert the rulers of the fort that an unwelcome guest was at their gates. The rest of this Indian fort is just as extraordinary.

▲ The fabulous Koh-i-noor — mountain of light — diamond was mined near Golconda in the early 14th century CE. After a long and colourful history that took it to northern India, Iran and Afghanistan, it has finished up in one of the British royal crowns. Once a vast 1,000 carats in weight, it has been re-cut many times to its current weight of 108.9 carats (about 22g). Legend has it that only a woman can wear it, since it will always bring disaster to a man.

▼ Golconda consisted of a walled city inside which were numerous palaces, mosques, government buildings, shops and houses. Dominating the city from its granite hill was Golconda fort. Other palaces and forts lay outside the city walls.

The shepherd's fort

Golconda lies on a hill to the west of the central Indian city of Hyderabad. Legend has it that in the 13th century CE, a shepherd boy came across an idol on the hill, which he took to the local king. The king constructed a clay-brick fort on the site, which became known as 'Golla Konda' – shepherd's hill – in the local Telugu language. In 1512, Golconda became an independent state. Over the next 62 years, its new Muslim rulers – the Qutub Shahi kings – rebuilt the fort in stone, as well as constructing a new city alongside it. New palaces, mosques and many other buildings were built, all cleverly designed to let in a flow of cooling breeze during the hot summer months. Water was piped into every building, and throughout the landscaped gardens, which contained many fountains and bathing pools. The entire fort and city complex was surrounded by heavily fortified outer walls about 11km long.

▶ The main fort of Golconda is built on a granite hill 120m high. Although now mostly in ruins, enough remains of the fort to show just how impressive it once was. Its granite walls stretched for 5km and had massive ramparts and other fortifications to defend it from attack. Specially designed parapets supported long-range cannons capable of firing 2.5km. Surrounding the fort was an immense city wall, which was entered through eight gates, protected by pointed spikes to prevent warring elephants from breaking them down!

Fabulous wealth

Golconda derived its importance from the diamonds and other gems mined to its southeast and then brought into the city for cutting, polishing and setting. In its heyday, during the 16th and 17th centuries CE, Golconda became famous for its great wealth: at one time, the 10km road from Golconda to Hyderabad was a vast street market selling diamonds, pearls, gemstones and jewellery to traders from all over India.

Such wealth and power attracted the attention of the Mogul emperors, who had invaded India from Afghanistan in 1526, and set up a powerful and well-administered empire that soon covered the whole of north and central India. During the 1680s, Emperor Aurangzeb (ruled 1658 to 1707) led his armies south and invaded Golconda. He captured the city, but the fort, however, held out until 1687, when Aurangzeb managed to trick his way in. After that, it gradually fell into ruin, its glorious past slowly fading from view.

▲ In 1687, Golconda finally fell to the Mogul emperor Aurangzeb, the last in a line of brilliant rulers. His successors struggled to keep his vast empire together, but their wealth remained immense, as can be seen in the fabulous robes and jewels worn by Sultan Akbar Shah II (ruled 1806 to 1837).

SUMMARY OF CHAPTER 2: THE GREAT AGE OF CASTLES

Defence

Castles were built not just to accommodate the local lord, his family and knights, but also to keep out those the lord wished to be protected against. They were defensive buildings designed to keep intruders out, with every element of their design and construction directed to this end. The walls were high, with few outer windows, and foundations were deep and thick, preventing the enemy from undermining the walls and causing them to fall down. Often, castles were surrounded by a moat, putting a stretch of water between the castle and the enemy forces. Many castles had high interior walls enclosing inner courtyards – the enemy might gain access to the outer courtyard, but further offensive operations would be required to seize the lord inside the main keep.

Motte castle from the Bayeux Tapestry

Attack

The construction of concentric castles in Europe in the later 13th century CE marked a new development in castle design. No longer were they purely defensive buildings, for the two roughly parallel sets of walls – the outer one lower than the inner – enabled defenders on the inner wall to protect the castle while those on the outer wall could rush out and take the battle to the enemy beyond the castle grounds. Further changes of design meant that the entrance to the castle became increasingly elaborate, with the simple, single gateway replaced by a heavily fortified gatehouse. All these changes were designed to make the castle impregnable, and its enemy vulnerable if they tried to attack.

At first, soldiers attacking or defending a castle used muscle-power to fire their bows and crossbolts, but the introduction of gunpowder, cannons and firearms during the 14th century CE gradually transformed castle design. Existing arrow slits in walls were altered to cater for handguns, while gunports were cut into the outer walls to allow cannonballs to shoot out towards enemy lines. The role of the castle was about to change.

Go further...

Learn more about castles: www.castlesontheweb.com

Take a trip to the many different castles around the world: www.castles.org/

Find out more about Welsh castles: www.castlewales.com/home.html

Castles of Britain and Ireland by Plantagenet Somerset Fry (David & Charles, 1996)

Eyewitness Castle by Christopher Gravett (Dorling Kindersley, 1994)

Why Are Castles Castle-Shaped? by Philip Ardagh (Faber & Faber, 2002)

Stonemason
Repairs and replaces old stones.

Conservation officer
Looks after old castles.

Medieval historian
Studies the period when the great castles were built.

Armourer
Restores and repairs medieval weaponry.

Computer programmer
Creates interactive games based on castles, knights and battles.

Website designer
Creates sites dedicated to castles.

Visit Chepstow castle (1067) in south Wales, one of the first stone castles in Britain. www.chepstow.co.uk/castle.htm

Explore the Tower of London – a 1078 stone tower, fortress, royal residence and prison. www.hrp.org.uk/webcode /home.asp
Tower of London, Tower Hill, London EC3N 4AB. T: 020 7709 0765

Visit Caerphilly castle (1268–1271) in Wales, one of the first concentric castles. www.castlewales.com/ caerphil.html

A ruined castle near the town of Kilgarvin, Ireland

CHAPTER 3

The end of an era

By the 1600s, the great age of castles had come to an end. Strong central governments in much of Europe and Japan guaranteed peace at home – and reduced the power and ability of local lords to wage war against each other. Castles were therefore no longer needed to protect local people from attack.

However, European nations still needed fortresses to protect their colonial and trading interests abroad, notably in the Americas. In the late 19th and early 20th centuries CE a new generation of semi-underground fortresses – such as France's Fort Douaumont, designed to withstand the heaviest artillery attack – was developed in Europe to defend national borders from enemy attack.

A few romantics built their own castles in an attempt to recreate a bygone age, but by the start of the 21st century CE, castles and forts belonged firmly to history.

Fort Ticonderoga

Not every fort or castle makes an impact on history. Many survive in local obscurity, rarely participating in events of national or international importance. One exception, however, is Fort Ticonderoga, an 18th-century CE American fort on the narrow strip of land between Lakes Champlain and George in upstate New York, USA. This fort made history twice and was attacked six times, all in the course of 20 tumultuous years.

▶ Fort Ticonderoga was built with wooden walls, filled with dried mud, and then covered with stone quarried from a nearby valley. Inside the fort were several buildings, including a barracks capable of holding up to 400 men and a large powder magazine. The star-shaped design of the fort left no blind spots where an attacker could hide, making it difficult to assault.

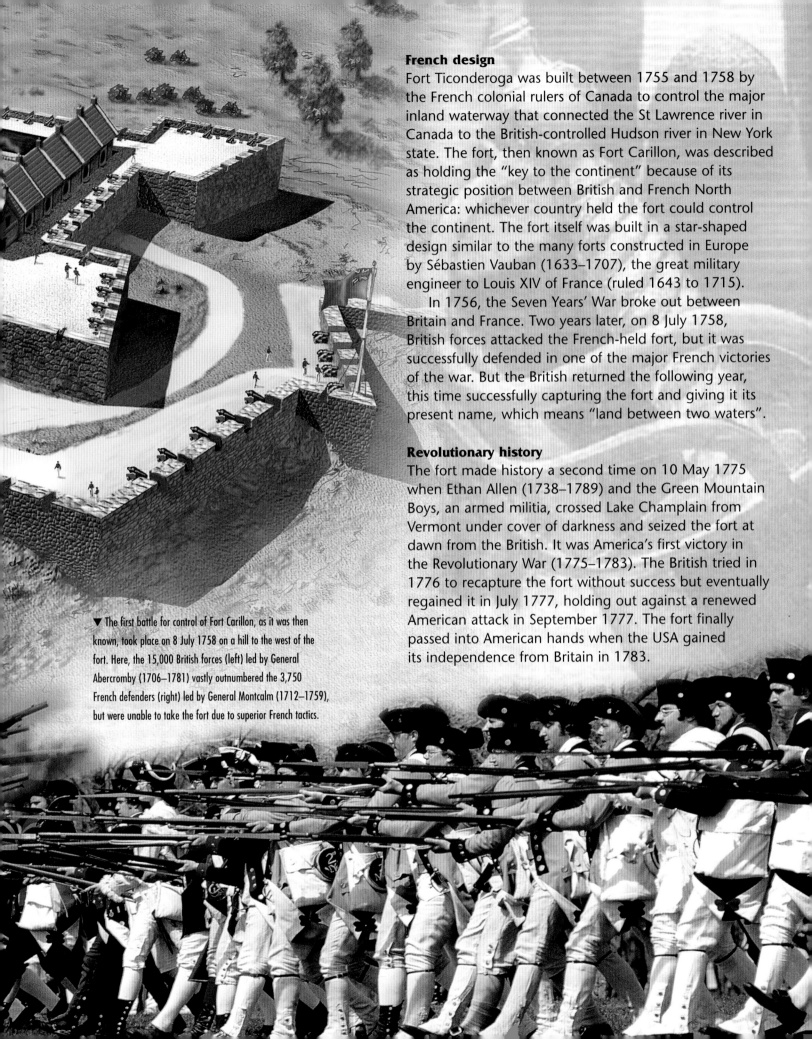

French design

Fort Ticonderoga was built between 1755 and 1758 by the French colonial rulers of Canada to control the major inland waterway that connected the St Lawrence river in Canada to the British-controlled Hudson river in New York state. The fort, then known as Fort Carillon, was described as holding the "key to the continent" because of its strategic position between British and French North America: whichever country held the fort could control the continent. The fort itself was built in a star-shaped design similar to the many forts constructed in Europe by Sébastien Vauban (1633–1707), the great military engineer to Louis XIV of France (ruled 1643 to 1715).

In 1756, the Seven Years' War broke out between Britain and France. Two years later, on 8 July 1758, British forces attacked the French-held fort, but it was successfully defended in one of the major French victories of the war. But the British returned the following year, this time successfully capturing the fort and giving it its present name, which means "land between two waters".

Revolutionary history

The fort made history a second time on 10 May 1775 when Ethan Allen (1738–1789) and the Green Mountain Boys, an armed militia, crossed Lake Champlain from Vermont under cover of darkness and seized the fort at dawn from the British. It was America's first victory in the Revolutionary War (1775–1783). The British tried in 1776 to recapture the fort without success but eventually regained it in July 1777, holding out against a renewed American attack in September 1777. The fort finally passed into American hands when the USA gained its independence from Britain in 1783.

▼ The first battle for control of Fort Carillon, as it was then known, took place on 8 July 1758 on a hill to the west of the fort. Here, the 15,000 British forces (left) led by General Abercromby (1706–1781) vastly outnumbered the 3,750 French defenders (right) led by General Montcalm (1712–1759), but were unable to take the fort due to superior French tactics.

Fort Sumter

At 4.30am on 11 April 1861, a cannon shot rang out across Charleston Harbor in the southern state of South Carolina, in the United States. Its target was Fort Sumter. The fort itself was insignificant, but that single shot started the four-year US Civil War that was to cost 600,000 lives.

The divided nation

Ever since the USA had declared its independence from Britain in 1776, the nation had been divided between the pro-slavery southern states, which needed slaves to work on their cotton and other plantations, and the anti-slavery northern states, which objected to slavery on moral grounds. The argument between the two sides came to a head in November 1860 with the election of an anti-slavery president, Abraham Lincoln (president from 1861 to 1865). The following month, South Carolina left the Union in protest, quickly followed by ten more states. Together the 11 rebel states formed the new Confederate States of America.

▲ The defenders of Fort Sumter had 48 cannons, but their supply of munitions was low. As a result, they were easily outgunned by Confederate cannons from Fort Moultrie, Castle Pinckney and from surrounding shore batteries.

Seizing the fort

As the USA headed for war, Confederate troops began to seize Union military arsenals and forts. In response, Major Robert Anderson (1805–1871), commander of US troops in Charleston, occupied Fort Sumter, a brick fortification on a small island in the middle of the harbour. But Confederate forces surrounded the harbour with heavy cannons and prevented ships from bringing more men and supplies to the fort. Anderson, 85 soldiers and 43 labourers, were besieged.

The fatal shot

When Anderson refused to surrender, the Confederate general, Pierre Gustave Toutant Beauregard (1818–1893), gave the order to open fire. The two sides battled it out until, at 2.30pm on 12 April, Anderson surrendered when Confederate shells set the inside of the fort on fire. The Union stars and stripes flag was lowered, and after a formal surrender ceremony, Anderson and his men were put on ships bound for New York, where they were received as heroes. The response of President Lincoln to the surrender was immediate: on 15 April he called for 75,000 volunteers to put the 'insurrection' down. The Civil War had begun, a vicious, divisive conflict that was to last until 1865.

▲ Fort Sumter was built between 1829 and 1830 on a shoal at the entrance of Charleston Harbor. It was named after General Thomas Sumter (1734–1832), a hero of the Revolutionary War (1775–1783). In recognition of its role in the Civil War, the fort became a national monument in 1948.

▼ Despite the heavy and lengthy cannon fire exchanged by both sides, no-one was killed or seriously injured in the 34-hour bombardment. At one point, the Union flag was blown off its flagpole by a Confederate shell. At considerable risk to his life, a Union sergeant climbed the flagpole to nail it back into place. The sergeant survived unscathed, although the flag was ripped to shreds.

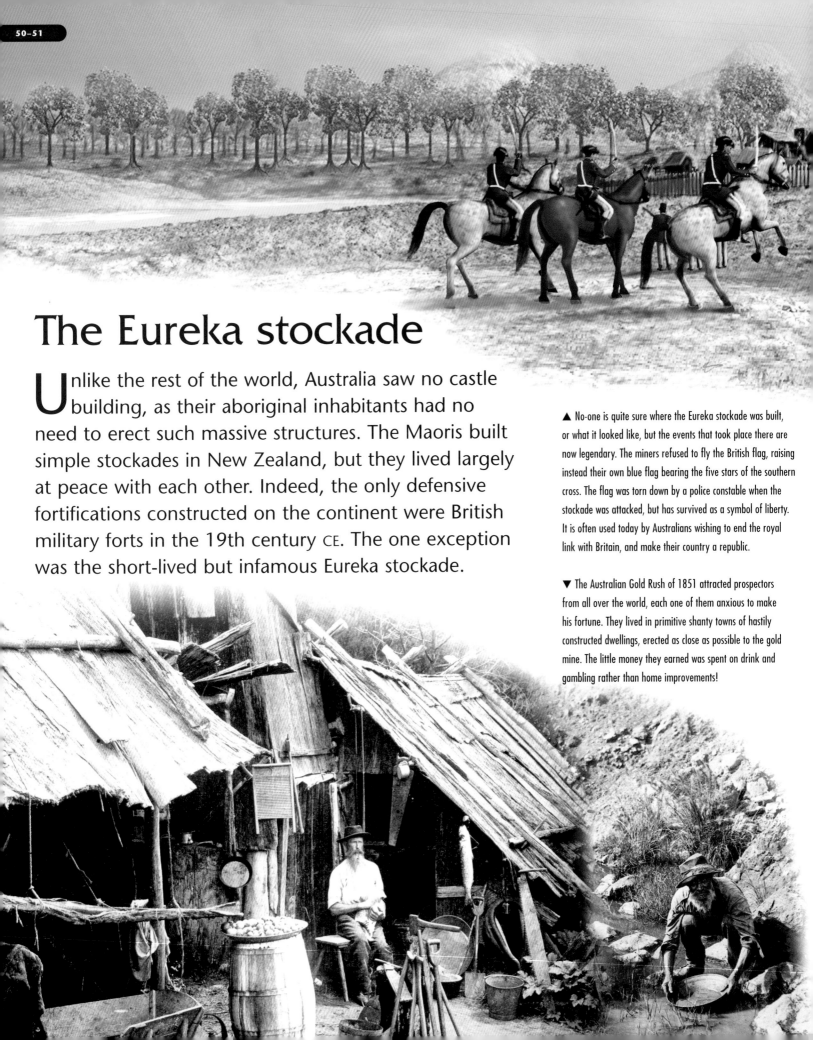

The Eureka stockade

Unlike the rest of the world, Australia saw no castle building, as their aboriginal inhabitants had no need to erect such massive structures. The Maoris built simple stockades in New Zealand, but they lived largely at peace with each other. Indeed, the only defensive fortifications constructed on the continent were British military forts in the 19th century CE. The one exception was the short-lived but infamous Eureka stockade.

▲ No-one is quite sure where the Eureka stockade was built, or what it looked like, but the events that took place there are now legendary. The miners refused to fly the British flag, raising instead their own blue flag bearing the five stars of the southern cross. The flag was torn down by a police constable when the stockade was attacked, but has survived as a symbol of liberty. It is often used today by Australians wishing to end the royal link with Britain, and make their country a republic.

▼ The Australian Gold Rush of 1851 attracted prospectors from all over the world, each one of them anxious to make his fortune. They lived in primitive shanty towns of hastily constructed dwellings, erected as close as possible to the gold mine. The little money they earned was spent on drink and gambling rather than home improvements!

Rebellion

On 1 and 2 December, the miners, led by Irishman Peter Lalor (1827–1889), built a simple stockade near the village of Eureka out of wooden pit props. The 150 miners inside the stockade armed themselves with rifles and sharpened pikes, determined to resist what they saw as the corrupt authority of the state. In the early morning of Sunday 3 December, troops surrounded the stockade. The miners opened fire, but they were no match for the troops, who killed 24 of them, injuring another 20. The miners' rebellion was over within 15 minutes, but the Eureka stockade has entered history as a symbol of workers' resistance to unjust authority.

The Gold Rush

On 12 February 1851, Edward Hargraves (1816–1891), a veteran of the 1848 Californian Gold Rush, discovered gold in the hills about 160km west of Sydney, New South Wales. Further discoveries led to the biggest field of all, at Ballarat, 120km west of Melbourne in neighbouring Victoria. Prospectors rushed in to make their fortune, many of them emigrants fleeing famine in Ireland and poverty in Britain. Few of them had any respect for British authority in Australia.

Showdown

The British authorities tried to control the rush by issuing licenses to prospect for gold, but corrupt officials abused the system and relations with the miners deteriorated. On the night of 6 October 1854, two miners tried to get a drink in the Eureka Hotel in Ballarat, but the owner refused to admit them and a scuffle broke out, the owner kicking one miner to death. A court let the owner off, so the miners held a huge protest meeting. When troops were called in to keep order, the scene was set for a showdown between the two sides.

▶ The Maoris of New Zealand constructed wooden stockades to protect themselves against enemy tribes. These simple stockades were stakes of local wood driven into the ground and then fastened together with ropes of twisted vines.

Fort Douaumont

World War One broke out in Europe in 1914. Millions were killed and injured, many along the western front between Germany on the one side, and Britain, France and their allies on the other. One of the main battles on this front took place in 1916, around the eastern French town of Verdun. The battle was bloody, but one part of it in particular was pure farce.

The importance of Verdun

Verdun lay close to the border with Germany and guarded the main route to the French capital, Paris. Because of its importance, the French had ringed the city with a series of heavily defended fortifications, including Fort Douaumont. The German army attacked Verdun and its forts in the hope that France would "bleed to death" and leave the war. France was determined to resist.

▼ The French army used a large number of heavy artillery pieces, such as this mortar, to repel the German attack on Verdun and its many forts.

▲ Ramparts, ditches, and rolls of barbed wire surrounded the entire fort.

▲ Douaumont, like all the forts around Verdun, was mostly underground. Originally built of stone with a covering layer of earth, the fort was later upgraded with a 2.5m layer of concrete placed directly above the stonework and a new 4m layer of earth placed on top of that.

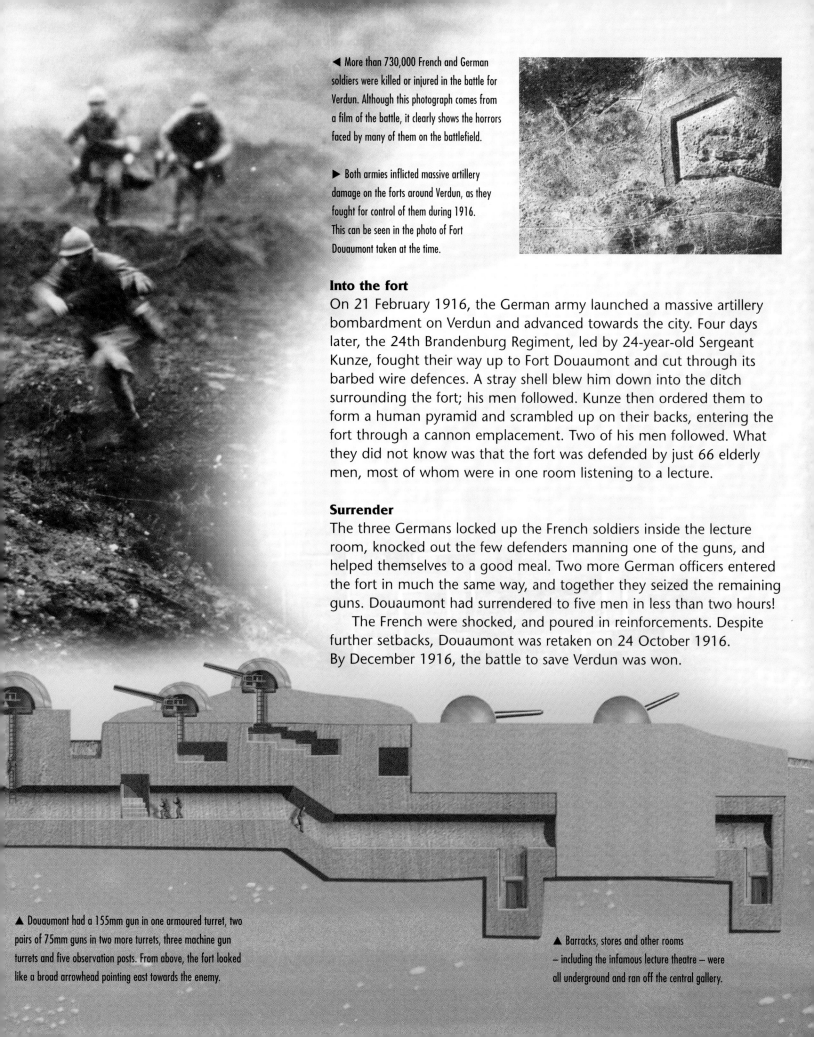

◀ More than 730,000 French and German soldiers were killed or injured in the battle for Verdun. Although this photograph comes from a film of the battle, it clearly shows the horrors faced by many of them on the battlefield.

▶ Both armies inflicted massive artillery damage on the forts around Verdun, as they fought for control of them during 1916. This can be seen in the photo of Fort Douaumont taken at the time.

Into the fort

On 21 February 1916, the German army launched a massive artillery bombardment on Verdun and advanced towards the city. Four days later, the 24th Brandenburg Regiment, led by 24-year-old Sergeant Kunze, fought their way up to Fort Douaumont and cut through its barbed wire defences. A stray shell blew him down into the ditch surrounding the fort; his men followed. Kunze then ordered them to form a human pyramid and scrambled up on their backs, entering the fort through a cannon emplacement. Two of his men followed. What they did not know was that the fort was defended by just 66 elderly men, most of whom were in one room listening to a lecture.

Surrender

The three Germans locked up the French soldiers inside the lecture room, knocked out the few defenders manning one of the guns, and helped themselves to a good meal. Two more German officers entered the fort in much the same way, and together they seized the remaining guns. Douaumont had surrendered to five men in less than two hours!

The French were shocked, and poured in reinforcements. Despite further setbacks, Douaumont was retaken on 24 October 1916. By December 1916, the battle to save Verdun was won.

▲ Douaumont had a 155mm gun in one armoured turret, two pairs of 75mm guns in two more turrets, three machine gun turrets and five observation posts. From above, the fort looked like a broad arrowhead pointing east towards the enemy.

▲ Barracks, stores and other rooms – including the infamous lecture theatre – were all underground and ran off the central gallery.

Romantic castles

By the 19th century CE, castles belonged in history. They had no military purpose, other than as army barracks or prisons, and many were falling into ruin, their stones plundered to use in other buildings. But one man had a passion for castles, which he indulged to extravagant excess. His name was King Ludwig II of Bavaria, a small kingdom in southern Germany. His monument is the fabulous Neuschwanstein castle, built not for war but for show.

▲ Ludwig II was king of Bavaria from 1864 to 1886. He spent most of his money sponsoring the arts, and building mock medieval castles and other follies. After he was declared mentally unfit to rule, Ludwig drowned in a lake close to Neuschwanstein.

Opera mad

Ludwig II had little interest in ruling his country. Instead, he devoted his life to art and music, in particular the operas of Richard Wagner (1813–1883), composer of the epic Ring Cycle of four linked operas and other works, whom he supported lavishly. Ludwig lived in a fantasy world – he eventually went mad – and dreamed of a castle inspired by Wagner's operas and their mythical, medieval settings. He designed his private rooms in Neuschwanstein entirely around Wagner's *Tristan und Isolde*, while the Singers' Hall was decorated with characters from *Parsifal*, one of the Ring operas.

Scene setting

Neuschwanstein was designed not by an architect but by a German scene painter more used to working on opera sets. It took 17 years and vast amounts of money to build, but although it looks like a medieval castle – complete with turrets, parapets, and battlements – it had no military function and is in reality a highly decorated modern home, with central heating and hot and cold running water. Ludwig died before his castle was finished – some parts are still incomplete today – but most of it was constructed by 1892, six years after Ludwig's death.

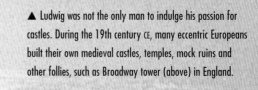

▼ Neuschwanstein castle sits dramatically on top of a rocky crag overlooking the peaks, valleys and lakes of the Bavarian Alps. Its dramatic situation makes the castle look taller and more imposing than it actually is.

▲ Ludwig was not the only man to indulge his passion for castles. During the 19th century CE, many eccentric Europeans built their own medieval castles, temples, mock ruins and other follies, such as Broadway tower (above) in England.

Understanding ruins

As we have seen throughout this book, forts and castles come in all shapes and sizes. Some have single towers, others vast complexes of walls, courtyards, gatehouses and moats. Some were once built of wood, others of brick and stone. Today, these castles are in various stages of repair, from perfectly preserved, well-equipped working and lived-in buildings to picturesque ruins. Visit a castle today, and you could be looking at a pile of stones, or asked in for tea!

Reading the ruins

It is quite easy to see how a castle operated if the building is still in a good state of repair, but even ruins can tell us a great deal about the life of a castle and its inhabitants. Huge foundations and thick, solid lower walls show the possible height of the main tower, while odd stretches of ramparts and battlements reveal something of how the castle was once defended from attack. Even a single ruined wall can suggest the groundplan of a building or the location of a long-forgotten barbican.

Into the drains

Historians can read contemporary records, such as official state documents and personal letters, to learn something about the history of a castle, but it is the archaeologists who reveal most about the life of the building itself. Using painstaking scientific analysis of everything from the mortar between the stones to the smelly remains in the drains, they are able to work out how the castle was built, where its stones came from, what its inhabitants ate and even whether they kept goats in the courtyard! They can tell us what happened to the masonry when the castle fell into ruin, as local people often used the castle's stones to build their own houses and other buildings.

Chance survival

So why are some castles ruined, and others not? The simple answer is pure chance. Many castles, such as the Tower of London, survived by changing roles – starting as a castle then expanding into a massive fortress and royal palace, serving as both a prison for enemies of the state and a stronghold for the crown jewels. Others, such as Maiden castle, survived for as long as their inhabitants did, and were then destroyed by their conquerors. Château Gaillard survived capture by the French king in 1204 but was then dismantled by another French ruler in 1603.

▲ The location of windows or a fireplace in a ruined wall shows how many storeys the castle originally had, and where its rooms were – even if the wooden interior floors have long since collapsed.

▼ This might look like a series of low stone walls, but archaeologists can examine these walls, and any pottery, bone, metal or other fragments they uncover around them, to piece together a picture of what the building was, and what it was originally used for.

◀ Little remains of Dunluce castle on the rocky cliffs of Co Antrim, in Ireland, but from the ruins it is possible to make out the rectangular great hall, the circular corner towers, and the location of the drawbridge linking it to the mainland. Your imagination will have to fill in the rest.

The castle today

Castles and forts have many different roles today. Some are still used for military purposes, but as barracks or regimental headquarters rather than for defensive functions – few would stand up to attack by modern-day artillery. Others have become prisons or storehouses. Many are private houses or, like Windsor castle, royal palaces. Most, however, are in public ownership, and are open to the public to visit. You can wander around the grounds, explore the keep, clamber over the battlements and even get locked in the dungeon!

Bringing the past to life

Walk through an empty castle and it can be difficult to visualize what life must have been like all those years ago. Many castles have therefore tried to recreate their past by filling their rooms with contemporary furniture, and stocking their weaponries with crossbows, rifles and cannons. Others have full-scale museums dedicated to the castle and its role in history, and publish illustrated guidebooks detailing what happened where, and when.

Guides take groups of people on tours of castles, explaining what a pile of old stones in the corner used to be part of, how many prisoners were drowned in the well and so on.

Living the past

Best of all, some castles stage re-enactments of historical events, such as battles, sieges and tournaments. Despite all the modern equipment, such as loudspeakers and burger vans, it is still possible to imagine that you are back in the past watching an enemy army storm the castle, or that the lord and his knights are staging a tournament, complete with jousts and other events, in order to improve their battle skills and impress their womenfolk. With colourful coats of arms, shiny armour and thundering horses, and with fanfares blaring from the sidelines, this is history brought to life as never before. Just for one day, you can be a French knight, or a Norman soldier, or an English bowman, fighting for your lord and your life.

▼ It might look like a scene from the Middle Ages, but these re-enactments of historical events take place in many castles today. The knights try to dress themselves and their horses just as their medieval predecessors did, giving 21st-century CE tourists a good idea of what a tournament or joust might have felt like for those who took part in them hundreds of years ago.

SUMMARY OF CHAPTER 3: THE END OF AN ERA

Why castles declined

Most people think that castles declined in importance because gunpowder and firearms made them easy to attack and capture. But gunpowder first appeared in Europe during the 14th century CE, and new castles were still being built 200 years later. The real reason for their loss of importance was that society became more peaceful and stable, so people could live safely in undefended country houses and stately homes without fear of attack.

Unwanted castles and forts soon fell into ruin, their stone removed for use in other buildings. Some castles became army barracks or military headquarters, others were converted into homes. Castles did continue in military use in some areas, notably along the land

Rifles from the Revolutionary War

border between Christian central Europe and Muslim Turkish-controlled southeast Europe, while new forts were built in areas of colonial conflict between the European empires, notably in North America.

Why castles revived

In the 19th century CE, castles began a new life as living symbols of the medieval world. Many people held a romantic view of that period: those who could not build a whole castle constructed a medieval folly or a classical ruin.

Today, castles and forts are vibrant buildings visited by thousands of people every year. They house museums of medieval life, and stage re-enactments of battles, sieges and jousts. They are lovingly cared for by stonemasons and conservationists, while archaeologists painstakingly excavate their grounds to discover clues to their history and life. Meanwhile, crowds of people wander around the great keep trying to imagine what it must have been like to live inside these great stone walls or face an enemy army camped outside. Castles are now as much a part of our lives as they were when they were first built.

Go further...

Find out more about Fort Ticonderoga in America:
www.fort-ticonderoga.org/

Discover the secrets of Fort Sumter:
www.civilwarhome.com/ftsumter.htm

Find out more about the amazing Eureka stockade:
http://users.netconnect.com.au/~ian
mac/eureka.html

Learn more about the Eureka flag:
www.ausflag.com.au/flags/
eureka.html

Discover what drove Ludwig II to build Neuschwanstein castle:
www.german-way.com/
german/ludwig.html

Sound or **lighting engineer**
Helps to produce historical re-enactments.

Prop and costume maker
Creates historical costumes and artefacts.

Architectural historian
Studies (amongst other things) 19th-century CE castles and follies.

Architect or **designer**
Turns ruined castles into modern homes.

Historian
Advises on the care and restoration of old castles.

Visit McCaig's folly, a Scottish 19th-century CE folly imitating the Colosseum in Rome, Italy.
www.follies.btinternet.co.uk/
argyll.html

Explore Castle Drogo in Devon, England, a 20th-century CE country house built to look like a castle.
www.nationaltrust.org.uk
Castle Drogo,
Drewsteignton,
Near Exeter,
EX6 6PB
T: 01647 433306

Glossary

archaeology
Study of the past using scientific analysis of material remains, undertaken by archaeologists.

bailey
Courtyard in a castle, also known as a ward.

ballista
Ancient, massive wheeled crossbow that fired wooden or metal bolts.

barbarian
Primitive or uncivilized person.

barbican
Projecting watchtower (linked to the gatehouse) over the gate of a castle.

barracks
Building used to accommodate soldiers.

bastion
Tower or turret projecting from a wall.

BCE
Before Common Era: a non-religious dating system in which 1BCE is equivalent to 1BC.

Bronze Age
Historical period in southern Asian, European and north African history, dating from roughly 3500 to 1000BCE, during which people learned to make and use bronze for weapons and tools; it was followed by the Iron Age.

catapult
Siege machine using a highly tensed arm which, when released, hurls a rock or other missile at an enemy's castle.

CE
Common Era: a non-religious dating system in which CE1 is equivalent to AD1.

citadel
Fortress built inside a town's walls, often at the highest or most secure point.

concentric castle
Castle with two roughly parallel sets of walls.

Crusades
Series of military campaigns, from 1095 to 1291, launched by Christian Europe to win back control of the Holy Land from its Muslim controllers. Those who went on crusade were known as crusaders.

curtain walls
The walls between the towers of a castle.

donjon
French word for a keep or tower.

drawbridge
Bridge over the moat that could be raised to prevent an enemy entering the castle.

feudalism
Social system in western Europe during the Middle Ages in which peasants and other vassals owed allegiance to their feudal lord in return for land and protection.

folly
Modern building in the style of a castle or other ancient monument.

gatehouse
Structure in the outer walls of a castle, usually consisting of two towers either side of the main entrance.

hillfort
Fortified hilltop surrounded by earth or stone ramparts, often containing a small village.

Holy Land
Land between the River Jordan and the Mediterranean Sea, in what is now Israel and Palestine, where Biblical events took place .

Holy Roman empire
Empire covering modern-day Germany, Switzerland, Austria, northern Italy and much of the Low Countries that existed from CE962 to 1806; the emperor owed his allegiance to the pope and was elected from among his fellow rulers.

joust
Combat between two mounted knights.

kasbah
Arab fortified house or castle.

keep
The stone keep was the centre of the castle, and the main residence of the owner.

knight
Mounted, heavily armed soldier who served his lord.

Knights Hospitallers
Order of knights first organized in Jerusalem in c.1070; their official name was the Knights Hospitallers of St John of Jerusalem.

ksar
Moroccan fortified village.

magazine
Building storing ammunition and weapons.

mantlet
Large mobile wooden shield protecting
assault troops and sappers in a siege.

mausoleum
Large stately tomb housing bodies.

Middle Ages
Period of European history from the fall of the
Roman empire in the 5th century CE to the start
of the Renaissance during the 15th century CE.

moat
Ditch filled with water, surrounding a castle.

motte and bailey
Simple wooden castle on a mound, with
a drawbridge connecting it to a bailey.

pike
Weapon consisting of a long wooden
pole, often with a metal spearhead
or sharpened end.

pilgrim
Religious or devout person who makes
a journey to a holy place.

pope
Head of the Roman Catholic Church
in Rome, in Italy; his government is known
as the papacy. The pope is based at the
Vatican – the papal palace in Rome,
attached to St Peter's basilica.

portcullis
Grid-like gate that can be raised and
lowered over the entrance to a castle.

rampart
Earthen embankment surrounding a fort
or castle, often strengthened by stone walls.

sapper
Soldier who digs trenches,
tunnels and other earthworks.

slingshot
A stone or other missile thrown out
of a sling at an enemy.

Stone Age
Long period of early human history when
stone was the main material for weapons
and tools; it ended after 3500BCE, at
different times around the world, when
the Bronze Age began.

terracotta
Hard, unglazed earthenware made from clay.

tournament
Mock battle designed to test knights.

trébuchet
Pivoting siege machine
used to hurl rocks
at an enemy.

Index

Acknowledgements

The publisher would like to thank the following for permission to reproduce their material. Every care has been taken to trace copyright holders. However, if there have been unintentional omissions or failure to trace copyright holders, we apologize and will, if informed, endeavour to make corrections in any future edition.

Key: *b* = bottom, *c* = centre, *l* = left, *r* = right, *t* = top

2–3 National Geographic Image Collection (NGIC); 4–5 NGIC; 7 Corbis; 10*t* Art Archive; 10–11 English Heritage; 11*t* English Heritage; 12*bl* Corbis; 12–13 NGIC; 13 Art Archive; 14*l* Corbis; 14–15 Kobal; 15*tl* Mary Evans Picture Library; 15*tr* Zev Radovan; 15*b* Corbis; 16*t* Corbis; 16*b* Corbis; 17*t* Bridgeman Art Library (BAL); 17*bl* Corbis; 17*br* Corbis; 18*t* Corbis; 18–19*t* Corbis; 18–19*b* Corbis; 19*tr* Corbis; 19*c* Corbis; 20 Art Archive; 21 Robert Harding Picture Library; 22*b* Art Archive; 23 Corbis; 23*tr* English Heritage; 24 Alamy; 24–25 DK Images; 25 DK Images; 26*tr* BAL; 27*t* Hutchison Library; 28*tl* Art Archive; 28*cl* HIP/Topham; 28*b* Corbis; 29*t* HIP/Topham; 29*bl* Corbis; 29*br* Skyscan; 30*bl* BAL; 31*tl* BAL; 31 Corbis; 32*br* AKG, London; 33 Corbis; 33*tr* Corbis; 33*bc* BAL; 34*l* Corbis; 34–35 Alamy; 35*tr* Corbis; 36*tl* Corbis; 36*bl* Corbis; 36–37 Corbis; 37*tr* Scala; 37*b* Art Archive; 38*tl* Art Archive; 38*cr* Corbis; 38–39 Getty Images; 39*t* Corbis; 41 Art Archive; 42*tl* Corbis; 42*b* Art Archive; 43*tl* Art Archive; 43*b* Corbis; 45 NGIC; 46*bl* Corbis; 46*br* Corbis; 47*b* Corbis; 48*tl* Corbis; 49*trl* Corbis; 50*bl* Corbis; 50*br* Corbis; 51*bc* Corbis; 51*br* Corbis; 52*cl* Corbis; 52–53 Hulton Getty; 54*c* Art Archive; 54–55 Corbis; 55*tr* Robert Harding Picture Library; 56*b* Corbis; 56–57 NGIC; 57*b* Corbis; 58*b* Corbis; 60–61 NGIC

The publisher would like to thank the following illustrators:
Mark Bristow 64; Robert McKoen and Daniel Shutt 30–31*tl*;
Steve Weston (Linden Artists) 1, 8–9 main artwork, 10–11 main artwork and *tr*, 22–23*tl*, 26–27 main artwork, 30–31 main artwork, 40–41 main artwork, 46–47 main artwork, 48–49 main artwork, 50–51 main artwork, 52–53 main artwork

The author would like to thank Melissa, Peter and Cee for all their hard work and enthusiasm in editing, designing and researching this book, and Gill for commissioning it.